I Can Read

Bumble's Missing Honey

HarperCollins *Children's Books*

This is Bumble.

He is a happy bee.

4

Bumble lives here,
in Honeysuckle House.

Bumble loves honey.
He finds pollen
to turn it into honey.

He pours the honey from a tap
and puts it into jars.

Everyone in Flowertot Garden
likes Bumble's honey.

Fifi uses it
to make honey cakes
and honey sandwiches.

Stingo likes Bumble's honey.
He wants to steal it!
Stingo and Slugsy make a plan.

Stingo and Slugsy look
to see where Bumble is.
Stingo uses a telescope.

Stingo can see Bumble.

He is at his house.

Bumble is tasting
his latest honey.
"Very good!" he says.

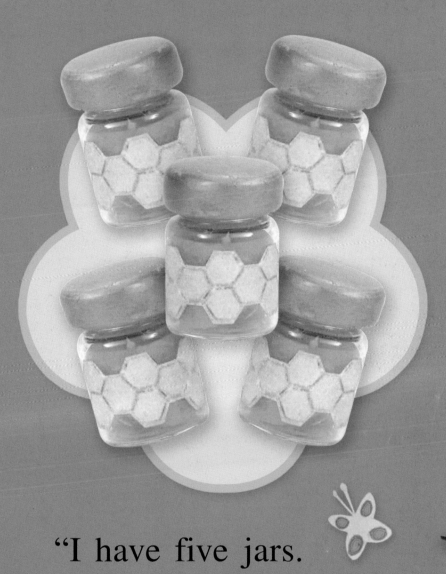

"I have five jars.
I will take one to Fifi.
That leaves four jars."

15

While Bumble is away,
Stingo and Slugsy sneak
into Bumble's garden.

16

Stingo and Slugsy
take two honey jars each.
They have all the honey!

Bumble gives Fifi some honey.
"Thank you, Bumble!" she says.
"I will make a honey cake."
Fifi asks for one more jar
so she can make
a hot honey drink, too.

Bumble goes back home
to get one more jar.

But when he gets home,
He sees no jars are left!

"That's funny," said Bumble.
"Where has my honey gone?"

Just then, Bumble sees
something funny on the ground:
a shiny, sticky trail!

Stingo and Slugsy
take the honey
back to the
Treehouse.

They do not know
that Bumble is following
their sticky trail.

Stingo and Slugsy start to eat
the honey.
"Yummy!" says Stingo.

"Stop!" says Bumble.

"You are eating my honey!"

Stingo tries to pretend
that the honey is his.

But Bumble knows that the jars
are the ones
missing from his house.

Stingo and Slugsy
give the honey back to Bumble.

But then Fifi arrives
with a honey cake.
"Everyone can enjoy
Bumble's honey!" she says.

31

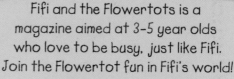